IN SEARCH of THE FAR SIDE

by Gary Larson

Andrews, McMeel & Parker
A Universal Press Syndicate Company
Kansas City • New York

ISBN: 0-8362-2060-9

Library of Congress Catalog Card Number: 84-71440

"Well, we're lost... And it's probably just a matter of
time before someone decides to shoot us."

"Charley horse!"

"Sorry to bother you, Sylvia, but your Henry's over here...and he's got my cat treed again."

"Auntie Em, Auntie Em!...There's no place like home!...There's no place like home."

"Dang! This can't be right...I can HEAR the stage, but I can't see a blamed thing!"

"I used to be somebody...big executive...
my own company...and then one day someone yelled,
'Hey! He's just a big cockroach!'"

Great moments in evolution

"Now this end is called the thagomizer...after the late
Thag Simmons."

Never, never do this.

"By Jove! We've found it, Simmons!... The Secret Elephant Playground!"

Obscene duck call

"Hey, wait a minute! This is grass! We've been eating grass!"

"Get a hold of yourself!...It was only a movie, for crying out loud!"

"Shoe's untied!"

"Ooo! Ow! Blast it, Phyllis! . . . Hurry up with them hot pads!"

"Hang him, you idiots! Hang him!... 'String-him-up' is a figure of speech!"

"Now let me get this straight... We hired you to babysit
the kids, and instead you cooked and ate them
BOTH?"

"See, Agnes?... It's just Kevin."

"Hathunters!"

"Yes. Will you accept a collect call from a
Mr. Aaaaaaaaaa?"

"The contact points must be dirty...just click it up and down a few times."

Primitive Man leaves the trees.

" 'This dangerous viper, known for its peculiar habit of tenaciously hanging from one's nose, is vividly colored'. Oo! Murray! Look!...Here's a picture of it!"

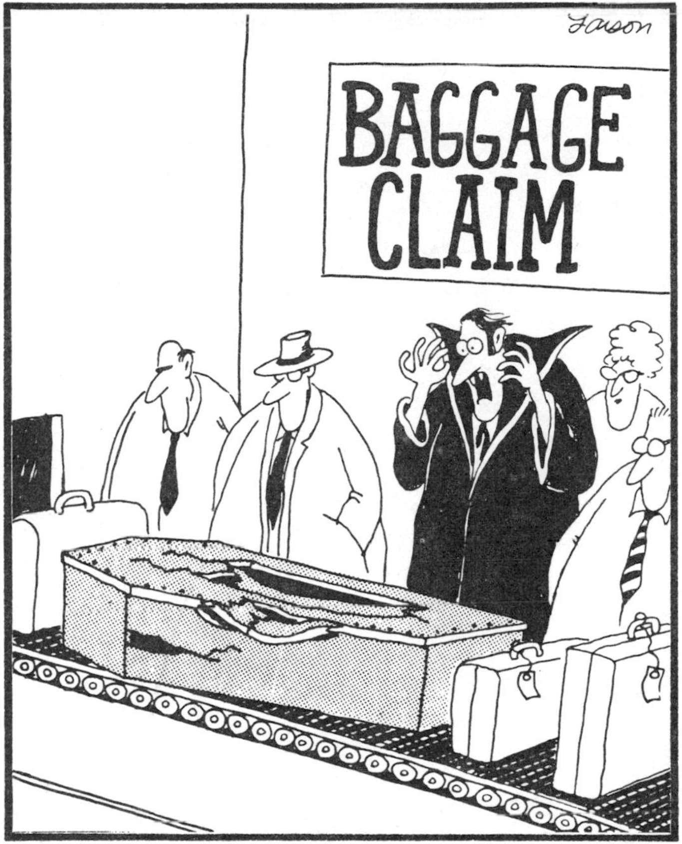
Larson
BAGGAGE CLAIM

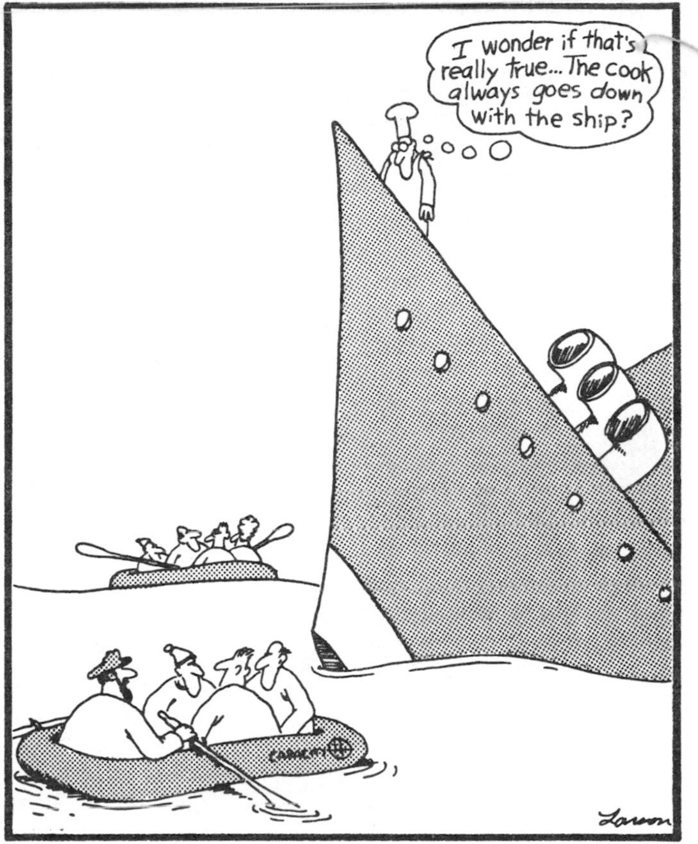
I wonder if that's really true... The cook always goes down with the ship?
Larson

Nature scenes we rarely see

Pet tricks on other planets

"Take another memo, Miss Wilkens...I want to see all reptile personnel in my office first thing tomorrow morning!"

"Oh, that's right! You DID have a hat...I believe you'll find it in the other room."

"Ernie's a chicken, Ernie's a chicken..."

Murray is caught desecrating the secret appliance
burial grounds.

Frances loved her little pets, and dressed them differently every day.

"Halt!...Okay! Johnson! Higgins!...You both just swallow what you've got and knock off these water fights once and for all!"

"Kemosabe!...The music's starting! The music's starting!"

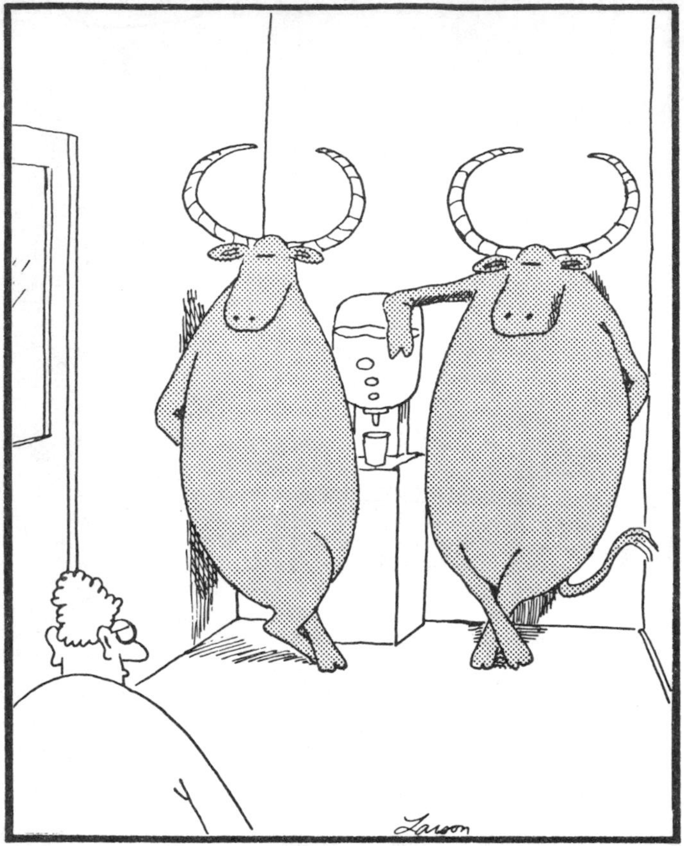
Larson

Water buffalos

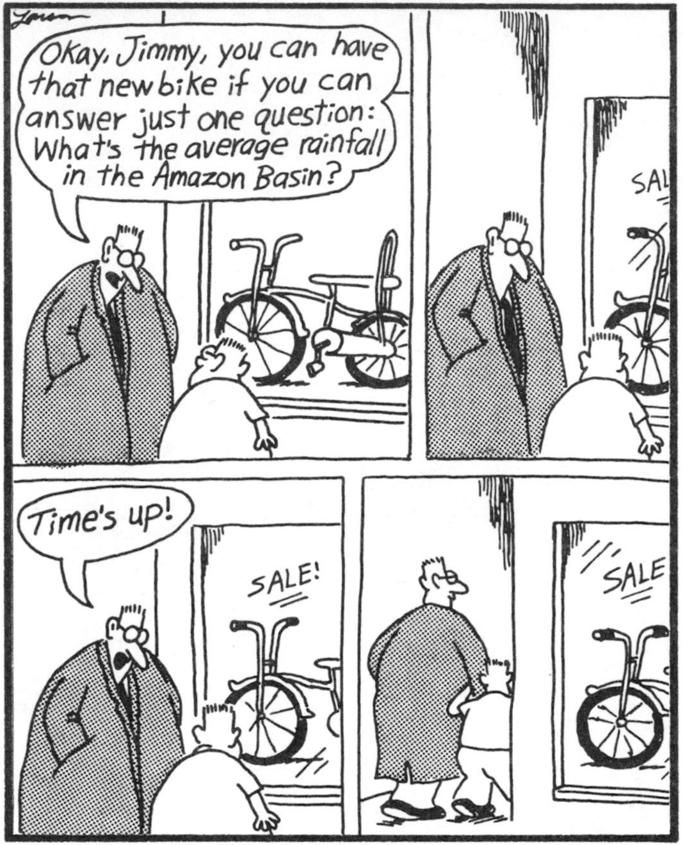
Larson
Okay, Jimmy, you can have that new bike if you can answer just one question: What's the average rainfall in the Amazon Basin?
SALE
Time's up!
SALE!
SALE

Games you can play with your cat

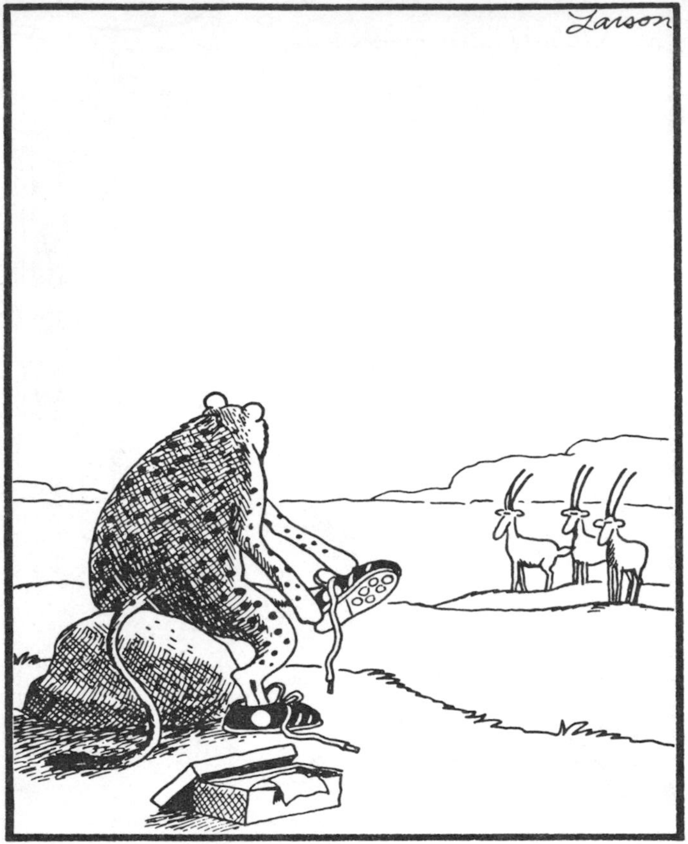
Larson

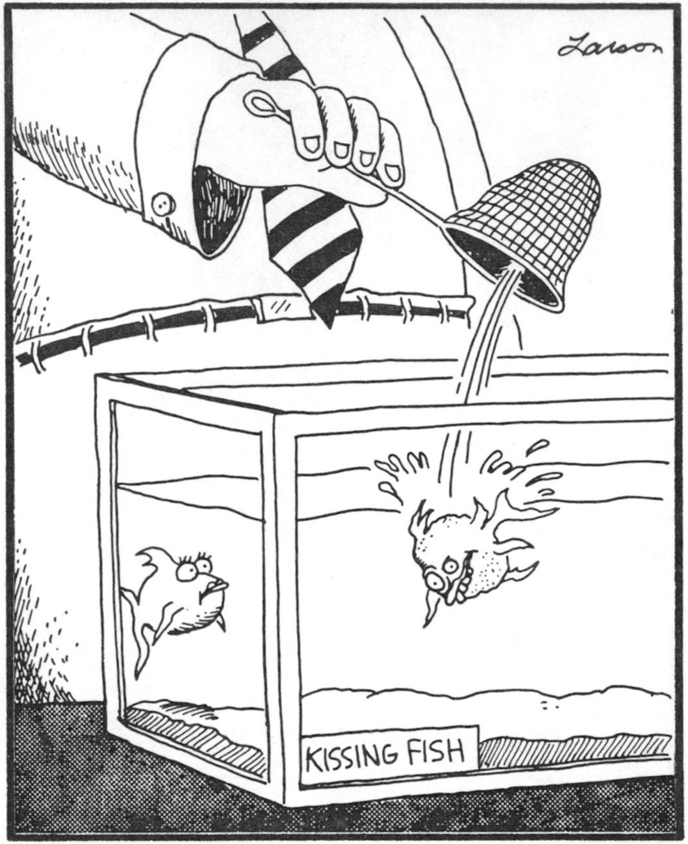
Larson
KISSING FISH

"Blast! This cinches it!...If we ever find it again, I'm gonna bolt the sucker on!"

And no one ever heard from the Anderson brothers again.

"Hey! You!... Yeah, that's right! I'm talkin' to YOU!"

"Hmmmm... Are the red ants right off the hill?"

"If we pull this off, we'll eat like kings."

Suddenly, Professor Liebowitz realizes he has come to the seminar without his duck.

"Okay, this time Rex and Zeke will be the wolves, Fifi and Muffin will be the coyotes, and...Listen!...Here comes the deer!"

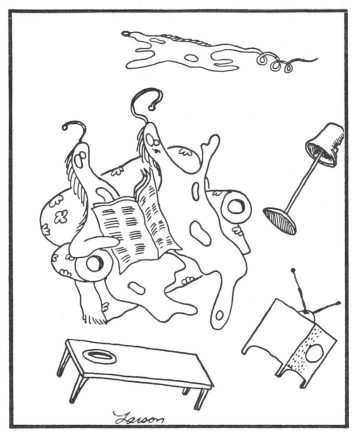

Things that live in a drop of water, and some of their furniture

"Yes, they're all fools, gentlemen... But the question remains, 'What KIND of fools are they?'"

"Fletcher, you fool! ... The gate! The gate!"

The elephant's nightmare

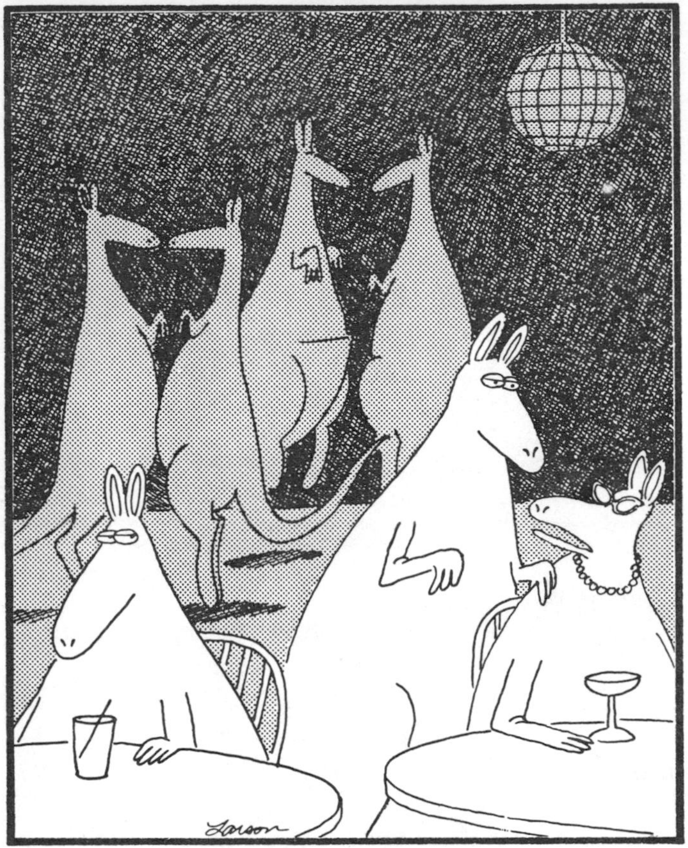
Larson

"No, thank you . . . I don't jump."

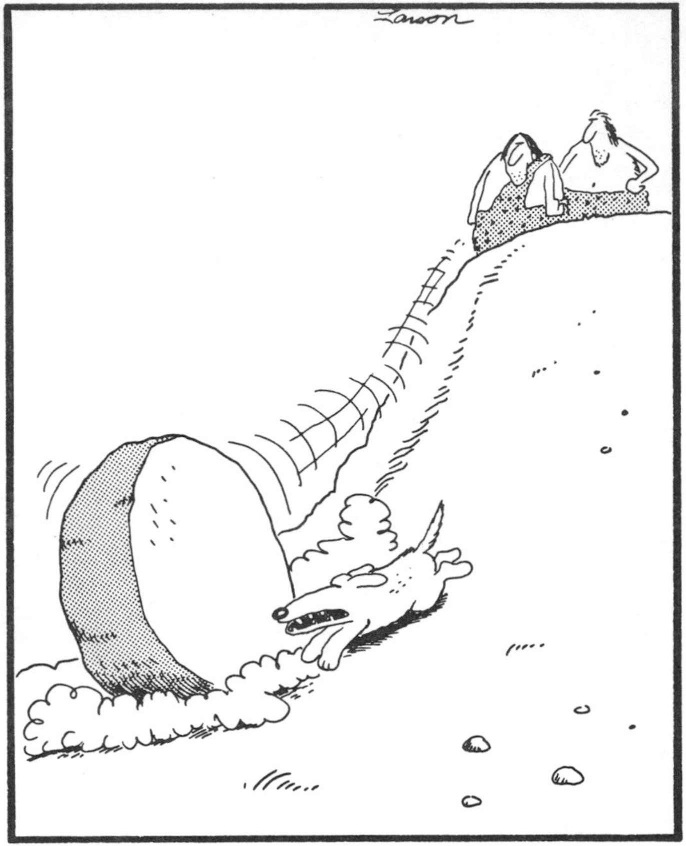
Larson

"Let's see... No orange... no root beer... no Fudgsicles... Well, for crying-out-loud!... Am I out of everything?"

"Dang!"

The Cyclops family at breakfast

"Well, hey... These things just snap right off."

"You meathead! Now watch!...The rabbit goes through the hole, around the tree five or six times..."

"Calm down, everyone! I've had experience with this sort of thing before...Does someone have a hammer?"

"Whoa, Frank...Guess what youuuuuuuuu sat in!"

With Roger out of the way, it was Sidney's big chance.

"Watch it, Randy! ...She's on your case!"

"Gee, Mom! Andy was just showing us how far he could suck his lip into the bottle!"

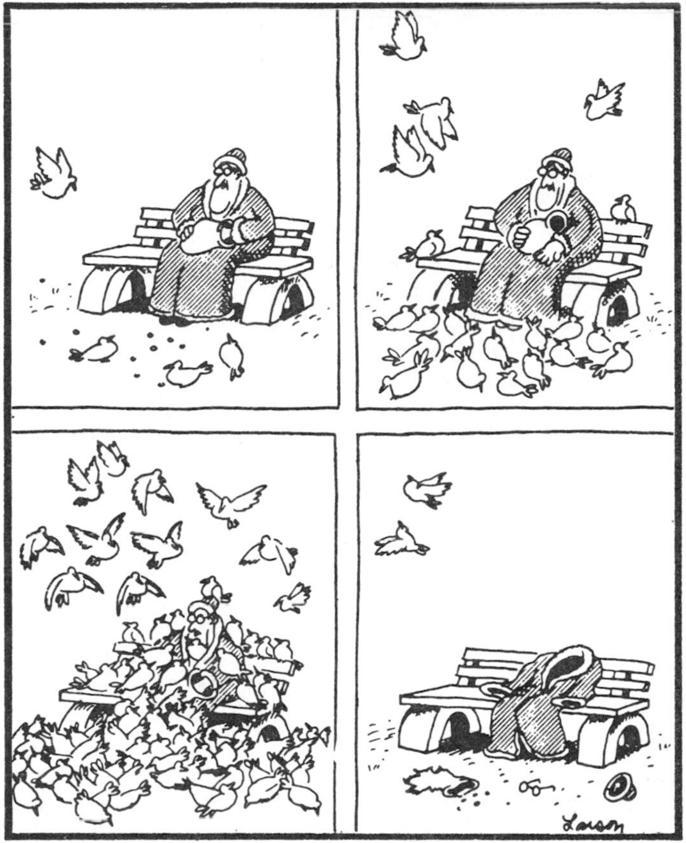
Larson

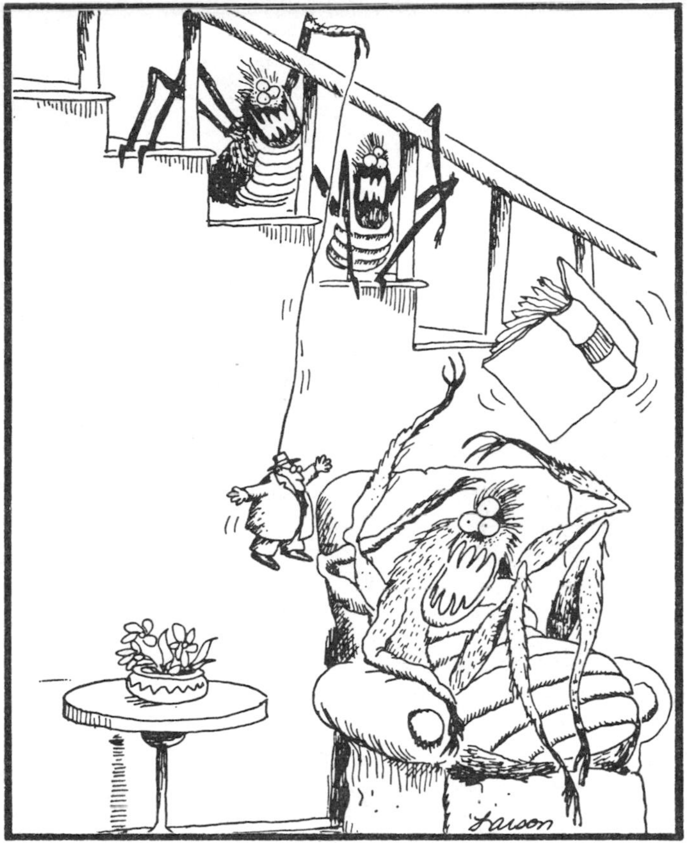
Larson

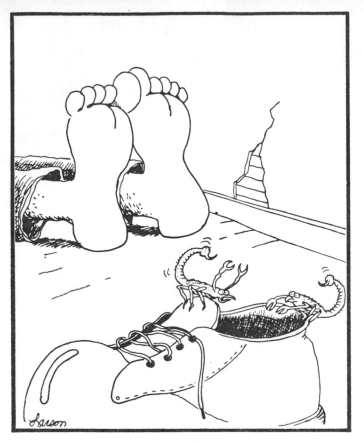

"There I was! Asleep in this little cave here, when suddenly I was attacked by this hideous thing with five heads!"

"Aha!"

"Pie trap!... We're in Zubutu country, all right."

"Oh hey! I just love these things!... Crunchy on the outside and a chewy center!"

"And now, Randy, by use of song, the male sparrow will stake out his territory...an instinct common in the lower animals."

"What?... Another request for 'Old McDonald'?"

The frogs at home

"You know, Sid, I really like bananas...I mean, I know that's not profound or nothin'...Heck! We ALL do...But for me, I think it goes much more beyond that."

"So now tell the court, if you will, Mrs. Potato Head, exactly what transpired on the night your husband chased you with the Vegomatic."

"Somebody better run fetch the sheriff."

"Andrew! Fix Edgar's head!...It's not facing the camera!"

"Carl! Watch for holes!"

"Mmmmmm... Nope... nope... I don't like that at all... Too many legs."

"Chief say, 'Oh, yeah?... YOUR horse ugly.'"

"Well, don't look at me, idiot!...I SAID we should've flown!"

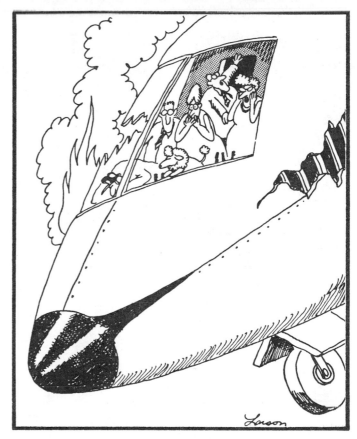

Suddenly, amidst all the confusion, Fifi seized the controls and saved the day.

"Lunch is ready, Lawrence, and...What? You're STILL a fly?"

"Relax, Jerry!...He probably didn't know you were an elephant when he told that last joke!"

Another great moment in evolution

"Curses! . . . How long does it take Igor to go out and bring back a simple little brain, anyway?"

When clowns go bad

"Well, what have I always said? . . . Sheep and cattle just don't mix."

"And I like honesty in a relationship...I'm not into playing games."

"Hey, buddy...You wanna buy a hoofed mammal?"

"There! Quick, Larry! Look!...Was I kidding?...That sucker's longer than the boat!"

"I've had it, Doc!...I've come all the way from Alabama with this danged thing on my knee!"

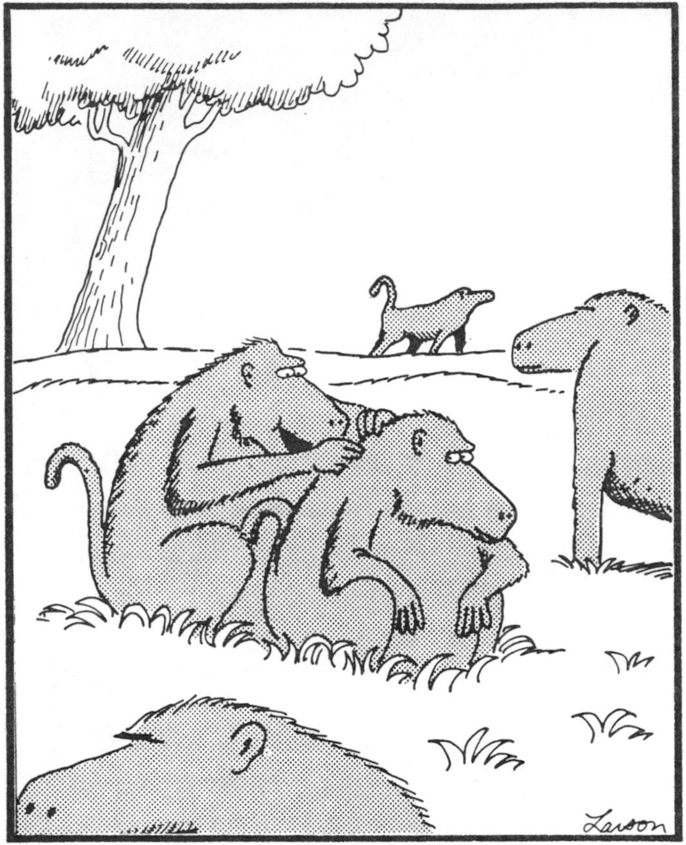
Larson

"So then Sheila says to Betty that Arnold told her what Harry was up to, but Betty told me she already heard it from Blanche, don't you know..."

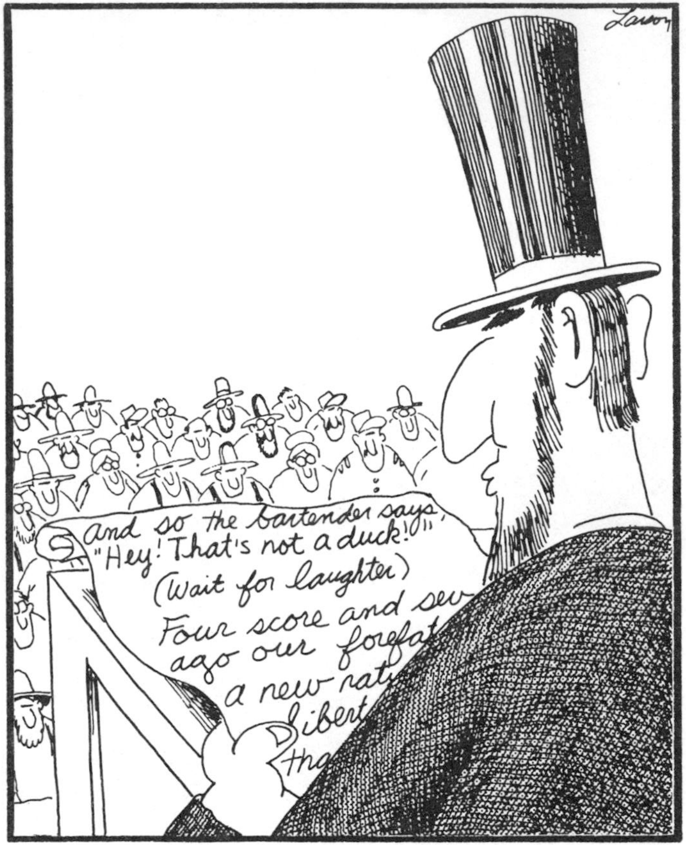
Larson
and so the bartender says, "Hey! That's not a duck!"
(Wait for laughter)
Four score and sev
ago our forefat
a new nat
libert
tha

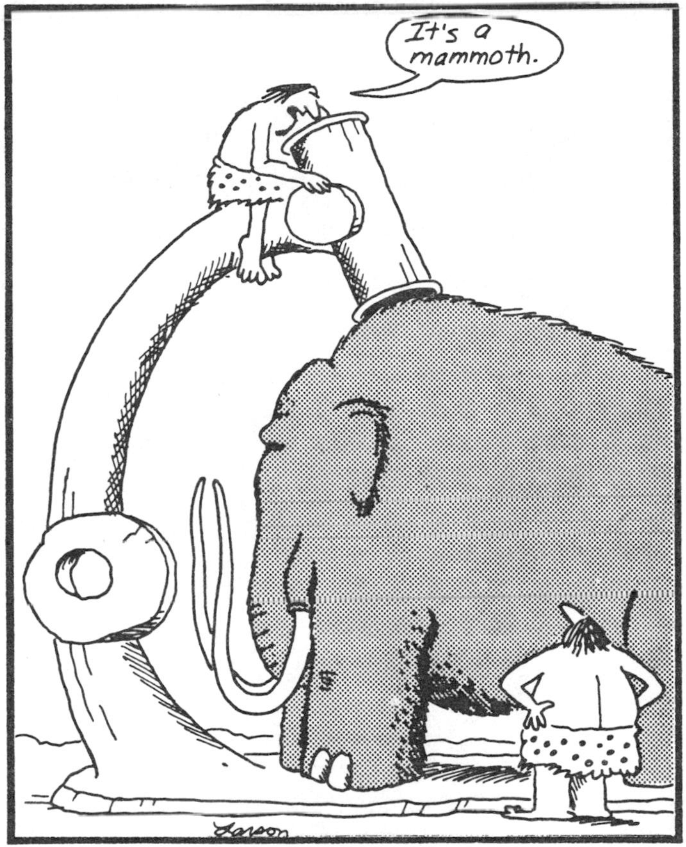
It's a mammoth.
Larson

Early microscope

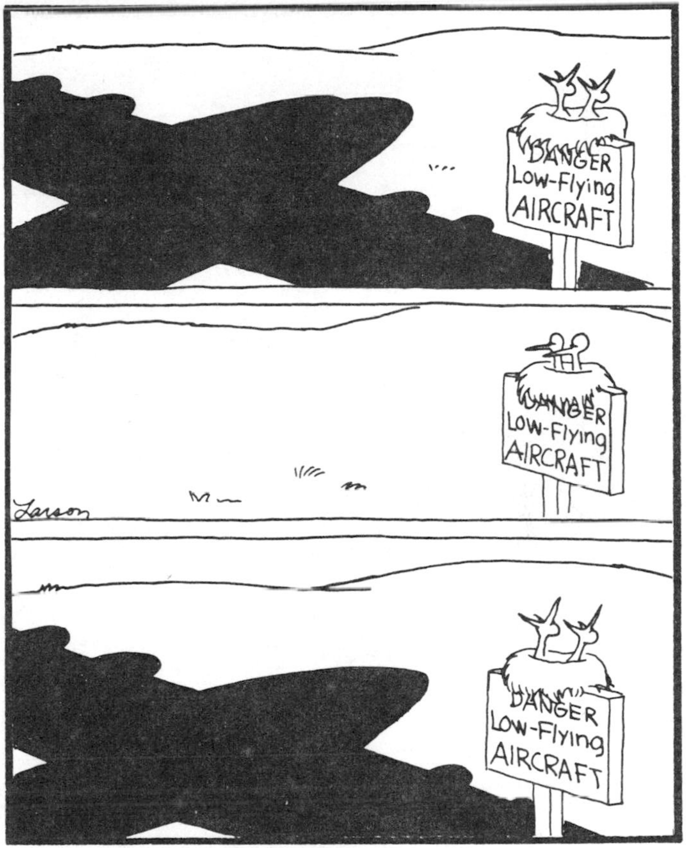
DANGER Low-Flying AIRCRAFT
DANGER Low-Flying AIRCRAFT
Larson
DANGER Low-Flying AIRCRAFT

Laboratory peer pressure

"Well, of COURSE I did it in cold blood, you idiot!...I'm a reptile!"

"Now, Grog! Throw!...Throoooooow!...Throw throw throw throw throw throw!..."

Cornered by the street ducks, Phil wasn't exactly sure what to do — and then he remembered his 12 gauge.

"Wonderful! Just wonderful! . . . So much for instilling them with a sense of awe."

The Portrait of Dorian Gray and his dog

Last of the Mohicans

"So, Andre!... The king wants to know how you're coming with 'St. George and the Dragon.'"

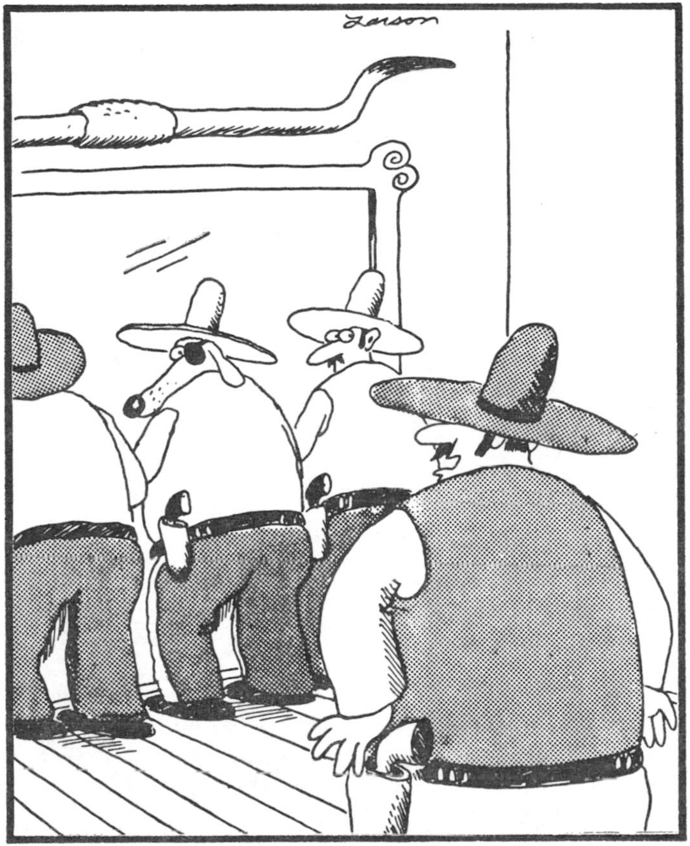

"Okay . . . which of you is the one they call
'Old-One-Eyed-Dog-Face'?"

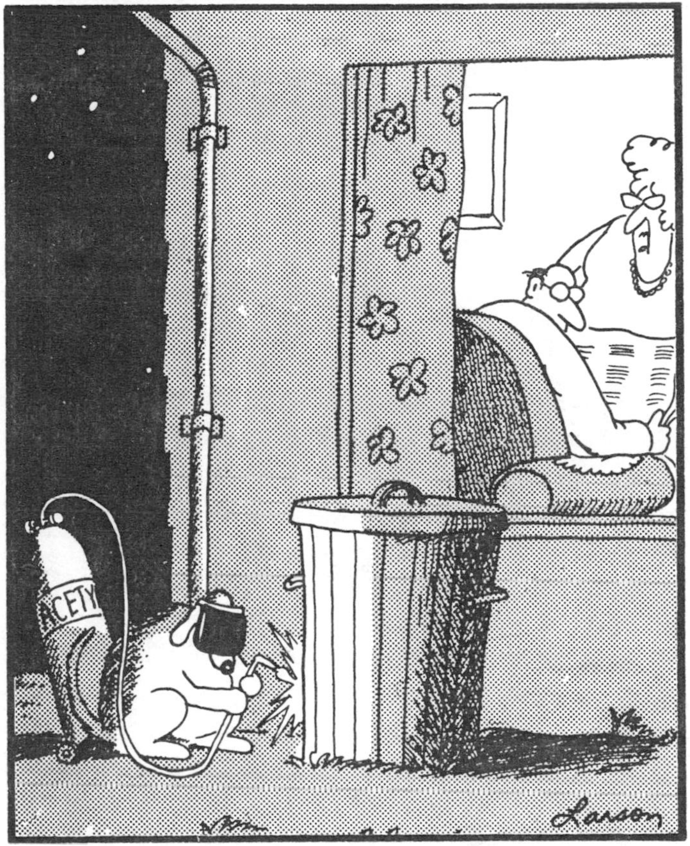
ACETY

"Vernon! That light! . . . The Jeffersons' dog is back!"

Psycho III

"Oh no, Elliott! Why? . . . Why? . . ."

"Well, they finally came... But before I go, let's see you roll over a couple times."

"Here's the last entry in Carlson's journal: 'Having won their confidence, tomorrow I shall test the humor of these giant but gentle primates with a simple joy-buzzer handshake.'"

Tarzan of the jungle, Nanook of the North, and
Warren of the Wasteland.

Carl shoves Roger, Roger shoves Carl, and
tempers rise.

On the next pass, however, Helen failed to clear the mountains.

"Aha! As I always suspected!...I better not ever catch
you drinking right from the bottle AGAIN!"

"I don't think I'll be able to tell the kids about
this one."

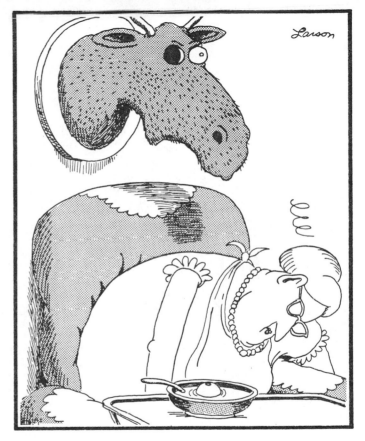

Buffalo Bill, Grizzly Adams and Pigeon Jones

"Uh-uh, Warren... The Williams are checking us out again."

"You call that mowin' the lawn?...Bad dog!...
No biscuit!...Bad dog!"

"I don't like this...The carnivores have been boozing it
up at the punchbowl all night — drinking, looking
around, drinking, looking around..."

"Tick-tock, tick-tock, tick-tock, tick-tock..."

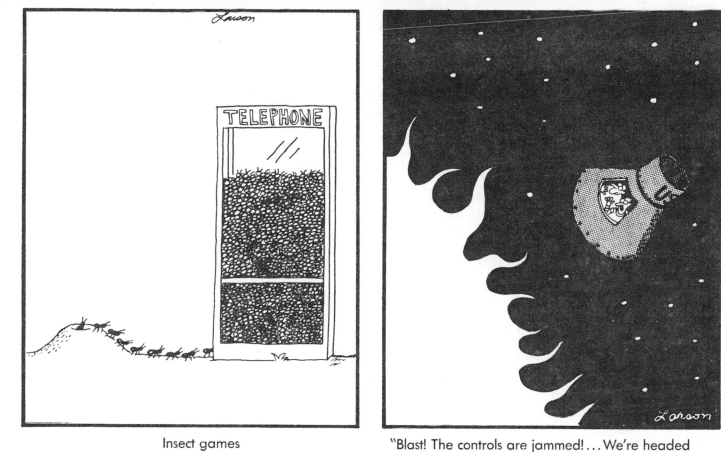

Insect games

"Blast! The controls are jammed!...We're headed straight for Mr. Sun!"

"Here he comes, Earl... Remember, be gentle but firm... we are absolutely, positively, NOT driving him south this winter."

Humor at its lowest form

"Oh. Now this is from last summer, when Helen and I went to hell and back."

"Wait! Wait! Here's another one...the screams of a man lost in the woods."

"There goes Williams again...trying to win support for his Little Bang theory."

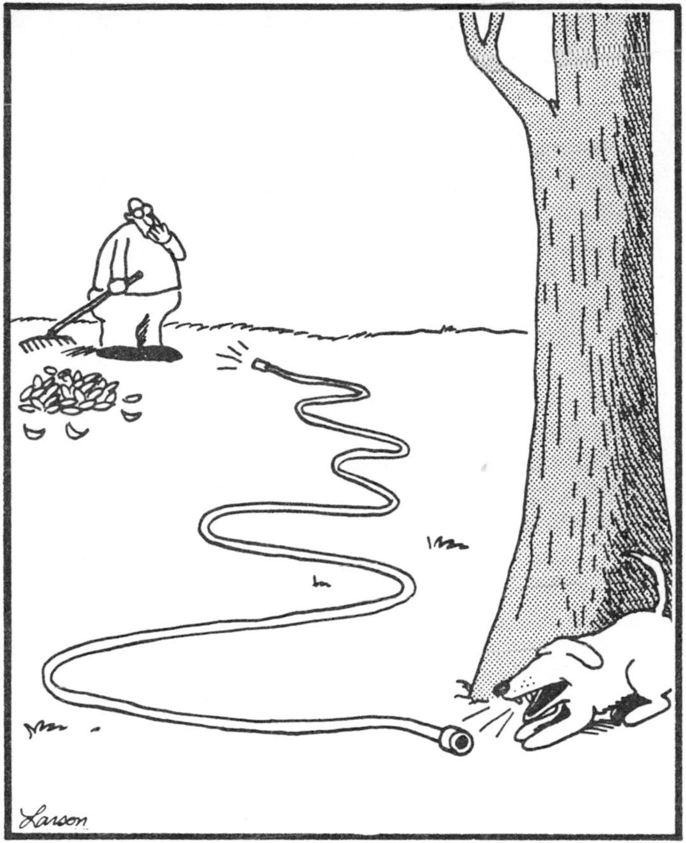
Larson

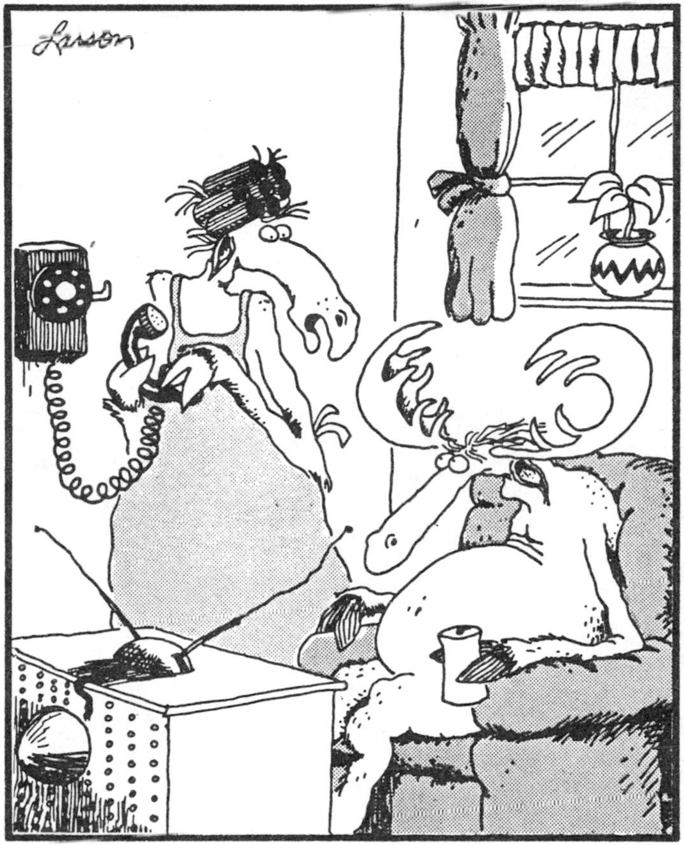
Larson

"It's the call of the wild."

"I guess he made it...it's been more than a week since he went over the wall."

"So, Professor Jenkins!...My old nemesis!...We meet again, but this time the advantage is mine! Ha! Ha! Ha!"

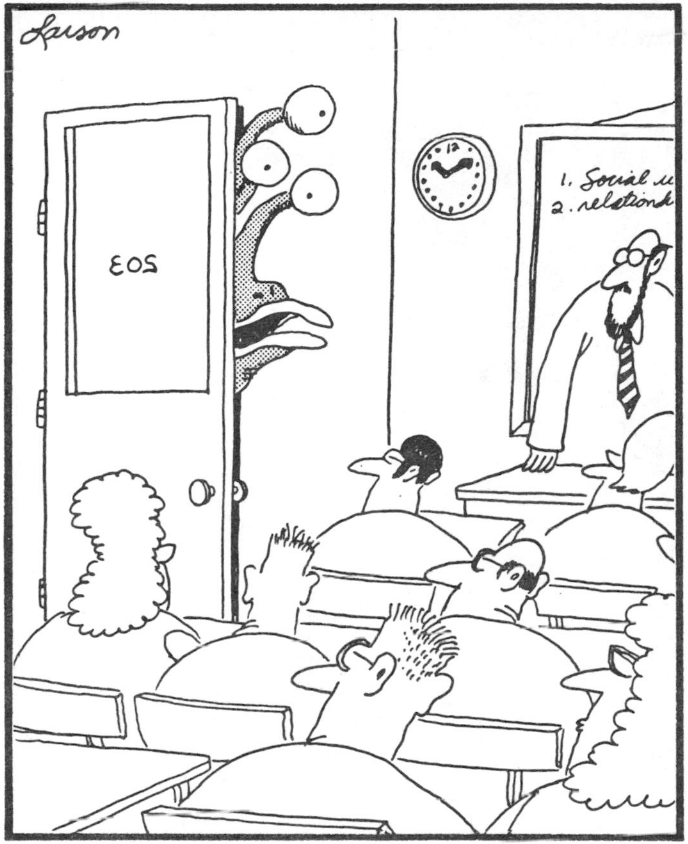
Larson

"Whoa!... Wrong room."

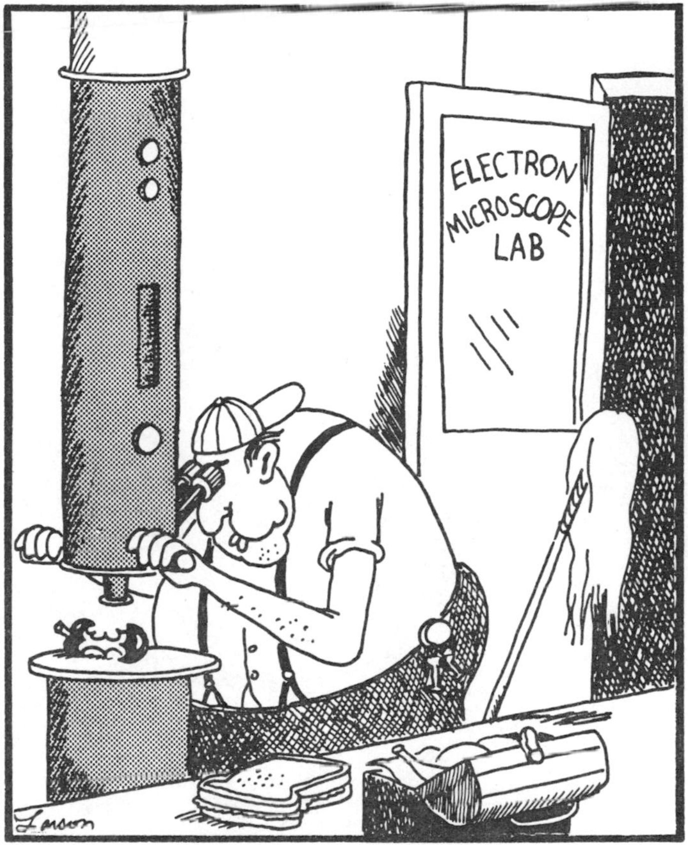
ELECTRON
MICROSCOPE
LAB
Larson

"I'll just take THIS, thank you! . . . And knock off that music!"

Darrell suspected someone had once again slipped him a spoon with the concave side reversed.

"Okay, here we go again...one...two..."

Never park your horse in a bad part of town.

On Oct. 23, 1927, three days after its invention, the first rubber band is tested.

Confucius at the office

"And you call yourself an Indian!"

"Hey! What's this Drosophila melanogaster doing in my soup?"

"Wait! Spare me!...I've got a wife, a home, and over a thousand eggs laid in the jelly!"

"Wait a minute here, Mr. Crumbley...Maybe it isn't kidney stones after all."

While Farmer Brown was away, the cows got into the kitchen and were having the time of their lives — until Betsy's unwitting discovery.

"I judge a man by the shoes he wears, Jerry."

"Boy, there's sure a lot of sharks around here, aren't there? ... Circling and circling ... There goes another one! ... Killers of the sea ... yes siree ..."

"Saaaaaay...I think I smell PERFUME!...Have you been over at the Leopard Woman's again?"

"So, Foster! That's how you want it, huh?...Then take THIS!"

Historic note: Until his life's destiny was further clarified, Robin Hood spent several years robbing from the rich and giving to the porcupines.

"Well, I'll be darned...I guess he does have a license to do that."

"Dang!...Who ate the middle out of the daddy longlegs?"

After 23 uneventful years at the zoo's snakehouse, curator Ernie Schwartz has a cumulative attack of the willies.

"The white whale! The whiiiiiite wh...No, no...My mistake!...A black whale! A regular blaaaaaaack whale!"

"Listen...You've got to relax...The more you think about changing colors, the less chance you'll succeed...Shall we try the green background again?"

"Thank goodness you're here, Doctor!... I came in this morning and found Billy just all scribbled like this!"

"Do what you will to me, but I'll never talk!... Never! And, after me, there'll come others — and others — and others!... Ha ha ha!"

"Oh, hey! Fantastic party, Tricksy! Fantastic ... Say, do you mind telling me which way to the yard?"

"Most peculiar, Sidney ... another scattering of cub scout attire."

"Aaaaaaa!...No, Zooky! Grok et bok!...Shoosh! Shoosh!..."

"Oh my gosh, Andrew! Don't eat those!...Those are POISON arrows!"

"For heaven's sake, Elroy!...NOW look where the earth is!...Move over and let me drive!"

"So! They're back!"

Trying to calm the herd, Jake himself was suddenly awestruck by the image of beauty and unbridled fury on the cliff above — Pink Shadow had returned.

"I've had it! This time I've really had it!...Jump the fence again, will he?...Dang!"

"Hold it right there, Charles! . . . Not on our first date, you don't!"

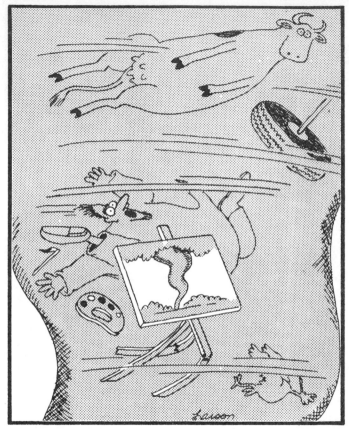

"That time was just too close, George!...Jimmy was
headed straight for the snakepit when I grabbed him!"

"A Louie, Louie...wowoooo...We gotta go now..."

Analyzing humor

" 'That's fine', I said. 'Good nose', I said. But no, you had
to go and hit the chisel one more time."

If you enjoyed *In Search of The Far Side* bet you'll like these two, too:

ONE SAMPLE JOKE

"Oh brother! Not hamsters again!"

The real reason dinosaurs became extinct

FOUR SAMPLE FUNNY LINES

■ "Anyone for a chorus of 'Happy Trails'?"

■ "My goodness, Harold ... Now there goes one big mosquito!"

■ "Yoo-hoo! Oh, yoo-hoo! I think I'm getting a blister."

■ "With a little luck they may revere us as gods."

(Aren't they good? And wait until you see them with Gary Larson's cartoons!)

FOUR SAMPLE FUNNY LINES

■ "Say ... what's a mountain goat doing way up here in a cloud bank?"

■ "Pull out, Betty! Pull out! You've hit an artery!"

■ "Oh boy! It's dog food again!"

■ "Rub his belly, Ernie! Rub his belly!"

(As funny as you find these lines, you'll love them even more with Gary's drawings.)

Available at your favorite bookstore!

Andrews, McMeel & Parker 4400 Johnson Drive, Fairway, KS 66205

© 1980, 1981, 1982, 1983, 1984
Chronicle Publishing Company

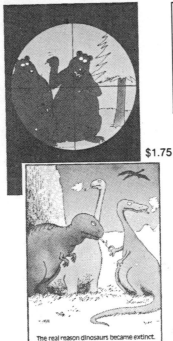